ROAD MAP

Saving Souls

DON'T GAMBLE WITH YOUR SOUL.

Which turn are you making? Which road are you taking?

HOPEFULLY NOT THE ROAD TO DESTRUCTION

Chuck Cotton

Road Map: Saving Souls
Copyright © 2024 by Chuck Cotton

ISBN:9781639451012 (hc)
ISBN: 9781639451005 (sc)
ISBN: 9781639451029 (e)

All rights reserved. No part of this publication may be reproduced, distributed, or transmitted in any form or by any means, including photocopying, recording, or other electronic or mechanical methods, without the prior written permission of the publisher and/or the author, except in the case of brief quotations embodied in critical reviews and other noncommercial uses permitted by copyright law.

The views expressed in this book are solely those of the author and do not necessarily reflect the views of the publisher, and the publisher hereby disclaims any responsibility for them.

Writers' Branding
(877) 608-6550
www.writersbranding.com
media@writersbranding.com

Contents

DEDICATION V
INTRODUCTION. VI
1. BIBLE. 1
2. HOLY SPIRIT 4
3. JESUS CHRIST 6
4. THE BLOOD OF CHRIST THE CROSS 9
5. SIN 10
6. SATAN/HELL 13
7. DEATH 16
8. LIGHT. 19
9. HEAVEN. 21
10. ANGELS 25
11. CONSCIENCE. 27
12. DISCIPLINE 28
13. MARRIAGE 29
14. ABORTION 31
15. HATRED. 33
16. BUSINESS. 35
17. AMBASSADOR. 38
18. THANKS 39
19. FAVORITES 40
20. CONCLUSION 43
21. SPECIAL RECOGNITION 45

DEDICATION

I dedicate this book to my wife, Joan, who has been my rock and partner for 56 years. She truly is my heartbeat and pulse. My daughters, Stephanie Jane O'Hara and Melanie Kathryn Obriotti, are included in this dedication as they, too, are part of my heartbeat and pulse. These women are the driving force in my earthly life along with the heavenly Father and his son, Jesus Christ. Someday, we will share our eternal life together.

Along with this dedication, I wish to thank those who have been part of my life since my childhood in Ridgway, Il, my alma mater, Southern Illinois University, and various careers at Marion High School, Balfour Company, Chubb Securities, Carriage Trade, JT and Charles Company, and VIP Limousine. Your friendship and loyalty to me is so special. Students, classmates, teammates, sales representatives and managers, fellow workers, customers, and family members are loved and appreciated. I thank each of you. God bless everyone.

Chuck Cotton

INTRODUCTION

My name is Chuck Cotton, 77 years of age, a Christian, an everyday citizen who has experienced a vast array of earthly experiences. I self-published my first book, GRANDPA'S NOTES in November of 2018 which was a lifetime of my maxims. I offer optimism and hope in sharing my philosophies, strategies and experiences which are aimed to help others excel and have joy in their lives. My book helps prepare them for eternity.

ROAD MAP is the successor book with primary subject areas in our lives supported by biblical verses giving you a guide to God and his son, Jesus Christ, our savior and what they have to say about them.

I do not expect everyone to accept all my maxims, but I do hope you will seriously accept God's word along with Jesus' sayings.

We are all God's children. Acts 17:26 says God made of one blood all nations of men to dwell on the face of the earth.

Regardless of who you are, religion, race, culture, creed, gender, class, demographic, we are God's children.

Sadly, many people on earth are gambling with their souls. Our soul never dies. Lost souls do not know where they are today.

ROAD MAP's message to you is DON'T' GAMBLE WITH YOUR SOUL.

Most people have never read the Bible entirely but occasionally glance at passages or become acquainted with scripture verses listening to preachers, religious leaders and educators. These people just are not focused on their souls, but on the daily earthly issues.

Satan is real and wants you to sin against our Lord. The devil wants you confined to his home, HELL itself. His spiritual fog surrounds earth. ROAD MAP bypasses the fog and gives you a clear road to heaven.

MY OBJECTIVE IN WRITING "ROAD MAP" IS SAVING SOULS.

We are in a diminishing spiritual world. Life passes so quickly; it is over before we realize it. Though we are living longer, we only have a few brief years left at best.

The world does not change.

God and Jesus Christ do not change.

The Bible does not change.

Satan does not change.

SO, WHAT DOES CHANGE? People

WHY? People are allowed choices. Such choices are influenced by spiritual or demonic forces. Our challenge in making such choices is whether the choice is centered on hate or love.

Ask the Lord to guide you with the right choice so his will is done. A simple prayer is please provide me strength, health, wisdom, boldness, and energy as I make choices. I am your servant.

ROAD MAP will help you discover ways to live the remainder of your earthly life. As a former athlete, I parallel ROAD MAP to my playbook. The Lord disciplines me when needed and always helps me when needed. He always helps me with taking the right directions with whatever road/weather conditions may be such as storms, fog, bad roads, traffic congestions, repairs. He always gives me the best routes or the best play. ROAD MAP will help those whose lives have taken wrong turns and put you on the eternal road.

Aging reality starts to become dominant in our lives. We have taken so much for granted in our lives without focusing of who we are and why we were created. God made heaven and earth and wants us to live in eternity with him. He loves us like no other. God threw Satan aka Lucifer and his demon angels out of heaven and will never let evil, sinful people in his kingdom. These evil spirits continue to destroy everything that comprises God's love for us and his earth and does everything to prevent our souls from entering heaven and eternity.

God sent his Son, Jesus Christ to earth to overcome Satan and prepare a way for each human being regardless of who you are, to enter his kingdom. Jesus's crucifixion and resurrection at the end of Easter week was the most significant weekend in history. Afterwards, Jesus's soul ascended into Heaven, carried by God's angels, and was seated on the right hand of God and by his side. Someday, when our life is finished on earth, we also will be carried by God's angels to heaven to be presented to Jesus Christ for judgment and an accounting of our lives. The Bible promises us if we believe Jesus Christ is the Son of God, mercy will be granted to us as we will enter heaven and join our loved ones.

The majority of people are gambling with their soul and are headed for eternal darkness and torment. I look forward to helping people navigate ways forward with ROAD MAP by penetrating your soul and bettering your life. Many people silently ask themselves, "How do I get to Heaven?"

The simple answer is giving yourself to Jesus Christ today. Trust him for your salvation. Repent your sins to Jesus and ask Jesus to forgive you of your sins, to come into your soul and he instantly will. I ask you to find a place of solitude to read God's word, the Holy Bible.

What is heaven like? Start reading John 3 & 14, James, Romans, Revelations 14,21,22, & 23, and finally Psalm 23. Your soul was made for God, don't gamble with your soul. Don't starve your soul. ROAD MAP will give you the right directions and turns. You can overcome any difficulty through hardwork, perseverance, and unquestionable faith and love in God, the Holy Father and his son, Jesus Christ, our savior.

1. BIBLE

The Bible is more realistic than all of the world's media. Read the Bible daily from Genesis to Revelation for strength and wisdom for the day and hope for eternity. God loves you. No matter who you are on earth, we are one blood.

"For ye are all the children of God by faith in Jesus Christ."
- Galatians 3:26

"And hath made of one blood all nations of men for to dwell on all the face of the earth, and hath determined the times before appointed and the bounds of their habitation."
- Acts 17:26

The Bible is the word of God. He inspired various followers to write under his holy spirit to guide our lives.

"All scripture is given by inspiration of God."
- II Timothy 3:16

"The words of the Lord are pure words."
- Psalm 12:6

"It is written, that man shall not live by bread alone, but by every word of God."
- Luke 4:4

"The earth is the Lord's and the fulness thereof: The world, and they that dwell therein."
— Psalm 24:1

"For the word of God is quick and powerful, and sharper than any two-edged sword."
- Hebrews 4:12

"God is a spirit; and they that worship him must worship him in spirit and truth."
- John 4:24

He does not have a body, nor is confined to one place. He has all the attributes of a person. You can ask him anything in the name of Jesus Christ. He never fails us.

"As we said before, so say I now again, If any man preach any other gospel unto you than that ye have received, let him be accursed."
- Galatians 1:9

"If any man shall take away from the words of this book of this prophecy, God shall take away his part out of the Book of Life, and out of the Holy City and from the things which are written in this book."
- Revelation 22:19

"If you abide in my word, you are my disciples indeed."
- John 8:31

"Forever, O Lord, your word is settled in Heaven."
- Psalm 119:89

No matter how far you have strayed, God is saying return to me, and I will return to you. He wants you to share eternity with him.

"The son of man has come to seek and to save that which was lost."
- Luke 19:10

"I have come that they may have life, and that they may have it abundantly."
- John 10:10

The Bible is given to us by the Holy Spirit's inspiration to guide our lives. The Bible reveals Jesus Christ, the bread of life, and the water of life, who will return to earth.

"Of that day and hour no one knows, not even the angels of Heaven but my Father only."
- Matthew 24:36

"Jesus Christ the same yesterday, and today, and forever."
- Hebrews 13:8

2. HOLY SPIRIT

God gives us the gift of the Holy Spirit to guide us. He promises to guide us and he will. The word from your God and Jesus Christ comes in truth and power, and from the Holy Ghost in joy.

"God is love whomever lives in love lives in God and God in them."
-1 John 4:16

"The fruit of the spirit is love, joy, peace, long suffering. gentleness, goodness, meekness, temperance: against such there is no law."
- Galatians 5:22-23

"God is a spirit: and they that worship him must worship him in spirit and in truth."
- John 4:24

"Behold my hands and my feet, that it is I myself: Handle me and see: for a spirit hath not flesh and bones, as ye see me here."
- Luke 24:39

"How God anointed Jesus of Nazareth with the Holy Ghost and with power: who went about doing good, and healing all that were oppressed of the devil; for God was with him."
- Acts 10:38 Read Acts 10:30-48

"Then Peter said unto them, Repent, and be baptized every one of you in the name of Jesus Christ for the remission of sins and ye shall receive the gift of the Holy Ghost."
- Acts 2:38

"That the God of our Lord, Jesus Christ, the Father of Glory may give unto you the spirit of wisdom and revelation in the knowledge of him."
- Ephesians 1:17

The early Christians started a spiritual revolution that shook the very foundations of the roman empire. In face of overwhelming opposition and odds, they remained bold, courageous, full of faith.

"They were filled with the Holy Spirit."
- Acts 2:4

"The Holy spirit prays for us."
- Romans 8:26

"Know ye not that ye are the temple of God, and that the Spirit of god dwelleth in you?"
- 1 Corinthians 3:16

"For as many as are led by the spirit of God, they are the sons of God."
- Romans 8:14

"Wherefore I say unto you, all manner of sin and blasphemy shall be forgiven unto men: but the blasphemy against the Holy Ghost shall not, be forgiven unto men."
- Matthew 12:31

"And whosoever speaketh a word against the Son of God, it shall be forgiven him; but whosoever speaketh against the Holy Ghost, it shall not be forgiven him, neither in this world, neither in the world to come."
- Matthew 12:32

"Now the God of Hope fill you with all joy and peace in believing that ye may abound in hope, through the power of the Holy Ghost."
- Romans 15:13

3. JESUS CHRIST

WE CAN SHARE Jesus Christ with a world that desperately needs to be saved.

"And we know that the Son of God is come, and hath given us an understanding, that we may know him that is true, and we are in him that is true, even in his Son Jesus Christ. This is the true God, and eternal life."
- 1 John 5:20

"Verily, Verily, I say unto you, he that believeth on me hath everlasting life."
- John 6:47

"He that believeth on the Son had everlasting life: and he that believeth not the Son shall not see life; but the wrath of God abideth on him."
- John 6:47

"The Father loveth the Son, and hath giveth all things into his hand."
- John 3:35

"All power is given unto me in heaven and in earth."
- Matthew 28:18

"For there is one God, and one mediator between God and Men, the man Christ Jesus."
- 1 Timothy 2:5

"I and my Father are one."
- John 10:30

"The Father is in me, and I in him."
- John 10:38

Road Map

"Grace be with you, mercy and peace, from God the Father, and from the Lord Jesus Christ, the Son of the Father, in truth and love."
- 11 John 7:3

"No one comes to the Father except through me."
- John 14:6

"For the Father judgeth no man, but hath committed all judgment unto the Son."
- John 5:22

"And hath given him authority to execute judgment also, because he is the Son of Man."
- John 5:27

"Therefore if any man be in Christ, he is a new creature: old things are passed away; behold all things are become new."
- 2 Corinthians 5: 17

"And he answering said, thou shalt love the Lord thy God with all thy heart and with all thy soul, and with all thy strength, and with all thy mind; and thy neighbor as thyself."
- Luke10:27

"And he said to him, thou hast answered right: This do, and thou shall live."
- Luke 10:28

"For we shall all stand before the judgment seat of Christ."
-Romans 14:10

"For it is written, as I live, saith the Lord, every knee shall bow to me, and every tongue shall confess to God."
- Romans 14:11

"So then everyone of us shall give account of himself to God."
- Romans 14:12

"I am the resurrection and the life: he that believeth in me, though he were dead, yet shall he live." " And whosoever liveth and believeth in me shall never die, Believest thou this?"
- John 11:25,26

"I am Alpha and Omega the beginning and the ending, saith the Lord which is, and which was, and which is to come, the Almighty."
- Revelation 1:8

" Keep yourselves in the love of God, looking for the mercy of our Lord Jesus Christ unto eternal life."
- Jude 1:21

"Lo, I am with you always even to the end of age."
- Matthew 28:20

4. THE BLOOD OF CHRIST THE CROSS

"In whom we have redemption through his blood, the forgiveness of sins, according to the riches of his grace."
- Ephesians 1:7

"Thanks be to GOD for his unspeakable gift."
- 2 Corinthians 9:15

God's love for us is absolute proof by giving his only begotten son to die on the cross who endured the penalty for our sin. The cross is the measure of God's love.

God's grace is exhibited when we bow before Christ in repentance and faith, we find forgiveness. Jesus paid the price for our deliverance by his death on the cross. The greatest gift in history was the cross. For there Christ suffered for us. Now he calls for compassion on others.

"For I am not ashamed of the gospel of Christ: for it is the power of God unto salvation to every one that believeth."
- Romans 1:16

5. SIN

"For all have sinned, and come short of the glory of GOD."
- Romans 3:23

Have you not repented of your sins you have committed?

Have you received God's gift of forgiveness? If not, invite Jesus Christ into your heart today.

Here are few biblical words, God has referred to as sin:

Idolatry, Witchcraft, Hatred, Emulations, Wrath, Strife, Seditions, Heresies, Envyings, Drunkenness, Revellings, Evil Thoughts, Adulteries, Fornications, Murders, Thefts, Covetousness, Wickedness, Deceit, Lasciviousness, Evil Eye, Blasphemy, Pride, Foolishness, Curseth mother and father, Steal, defraud, fake witness, Kill, Excess Wine, Unjust, Extortioners, Despiteful, Proud, Maliciousness, Full of envy, Deceit, Malignity, Back Biters, Haters of GOD.

"For the wages of sin is death; but the gift of God is eternal life through Jesus Christ our Lord."
-Romans 6:23

"Who knowing the judgment of God, that they which commit such things are worthy of death, not only do the same, but have pleasure in them that do them."
- Romans 1:32

"There is no fear of God before their eyes."
- Romans 3:18

Road Map

"Blessed is the man that endureth temptation; for when he is tried, he shall receive the crown of life which the Lord hath promised to them that love him."
- James 1:12

"If we confess our sins, he is faithful and just to forgive us our sins, and to cleanse us from all unrighteousness."
-1 John 1:9

"All that is in the world-e lust of the flesh, the lust of the eyes, and the pride of life is not of the Father but is of the world."
-1 John 2:16

"Likewise, I say unto you, there is joy in the presence of angels of God over one sinner that repenteth."
-Luke 15:10

"All things are open to the eyes of him to whom we must give account."
- Hebrews 4:13

"Thy sins are forgiven."
- Luke 7:48

"Thy faith hath saved thee."
-Luke 7:50

"But that ye may know that the son of man hath power on earth to forgive sins."
-Matthew 9:6

"And their sins and iniquities will I remember no more."
-Hebrews 10:17

"In whom we have redemption through his blood, the forgiveness of sins, according to the riches of his grace."
-Ephesians 1:7

"and thou shall love the Lord thy God with all thy heart, and with all thy soul, and with all thy mind." This is the first commandment.

"and the second is like, namely, this, thou shall love they neighbor as thyself. There is none other commandment greater than these."
-Mark 12:30 & 31

"Repent: for the kingdom of heaven is at hand."
-Matthew 4:17

"My soul shall be joyful in the Lord."
-Psalm 35:9

ASK JESUS DAILY FOR FORGIVENESS OF SINS.

6. SATAN/HELL

PREPARE TO DEFEND EVIL AT ANY MOMENT.

Never forget, Satan is a very powerful spiritual being.

1 Peter 5:8 & 9 says your enemy, the devil, prowls around like a roaring lion looking for someone to devour. Resist him.

Satan is a defeated foe. Jesus's resurrection overcame the power of sin and death. Someday, Satan will be chained and bound destroyed for eternity.

Revelation 12 describes the story of Satan being casted out of heaven. Satan and his angels rebelled against God. Michael and his angels fought the devil's angels and won. There was never again to be a place in heaven for them or evilness of any kind. Satan knows his time is short here on earth and attempts to devour everything God has made and Jesus Christ himself.

"Put on the whole armour of god that ye may be able to stand against the wiles of the devil."
-Ephesians 6:11

"But the Lord is faithful, who shall stablish you and keep you from evil."
- ll Thessalonians 3:3

"Resist the devil and he will flee from you. Draw near to God and he will draw near to you."
-James 4:7 & 8

"Wait on the Lord and he shall strengthen your heart."
-Psalm 27:14

"And no marvel; for satan himself is transformed into an angel of light."
-ll Corinthians 11:14

"For there are false apostles, deceitful workers, transforming themselves into the apostles of Christ."
-ll Corinthians 11:13

"He is antichrist that denieth the Father and the Son."
-l John 2:22

"Even now are there many antichrists."
-l John 2:18

"Beware of false prophets which come to you in sheep's clothing, but inwardly, they are ravening wolves."
-Matthew 7:15

"Depart from me, ye cursed, into everlasting fire, prepared for the devil and his angels."
-Matthew 25:41

"The Lord preserveth all them that love him: but all the wicked will he destroy."
-Psalm 145:20

"And these shall go away into everlasting punishment: but the righteous into life eternal."
-Matthew 25:46

"Hold thy peace and come out of him."
-Luke 4:35

"Get thee behind me, satan, for it is written, thou shall worship the Lord thy God, and him only shalt thou serve."
-Luke 4:8

"It is said thou shall not tempt the Lord thy God."
-Luke 4:12

"...Shall be cast out into outer darkness: there shall be weeping and gnashing of teeth."
-Matthew 8:12

"And he shall cast them into a furnace of fire: thee shall be wailing and gnashing of teeth."
-Matthew 13:42

"The Son of Man shall send forth his angels, and they shall gather out of his kingdom all things that offend, and them which do iniquity."

"And the Lord shall deliver me from every evil work, and will preserve me unto his heavenly kingdom. To whom be glory for ever and ever. AMEN."
-ll Timothy 4:18

"Now the spirit speaketh expressingly, that in the latter times, some shall depart from the faith, giving heed to seducing spirits, and doctrines of devils:"

"Speaking lies in hypocrisy; having their conscience seared with a hot iron."
-l Timothy 4: 1 & 2

"For we hear that there are some which walk among you disorderly, working not at all, but are busybodies."
-ll Thessalonians 3:11

"That he no longer should live the rest of his time in the flesh to the lusts of many, but to the will of God."
- l Peter 4:2

7. DEATH

At the moment of death, angels carry the soul directly to heaven. Along with the way, the soul may enter the valley of the shadow of death, but the angels will always accompany the soul all the way. The burdens of life are over. Life is short and quick here on earth. The years have passed and earthly life is almost over. This life will not continue. Live instead, with eternity in view. Follow Jesus Christ and at life's end, you will be able to say, "No regrets".

"The Lord is my shepherd; I shall not want.

"He maketh me to lie down in green pastures; he leadeth me beside the still waters.

"He restoreth my soul: He leadeth me in the paths of righteousness for his name's sake. "Yea, though I walk through the valley of the shadow of death, I will fear no evil: for thou art with me; thy rod and thy staff they comfort me.

"Thou preparest a table before me in the presence of mine enemies: thou anointest my head with oil; my cup runneth over.

"Surely goodness and mercy shall follow me all the days of my life: and I will dwell in the house of the Lord forever."
-Psalm 23:1-6

"For God so loveth the world that he gave his only begotten son, that whoever believes in him shall not perish but have eternal life."
-John 3:16

"I am not alone because the Father is with me."
-John 16:32

"But I have trusted in thy mercy, my heart shall rejoice in thy salvation."
-Psalm 13:5

"When a wicked man dieth, his expectation shall perish; and the hope of unjust men perisheth."
-Proverbs 11:7

"Verily, Verily, I say unto you, if a man keep my saying, he shall never see death."
-John 8:51

"For I am now ready to be offered, and the time of my departure is at hand. I have fought a good fight, I have finished my course, I have kept the faith."

"Henceforth, there is laid up for me a crown of righteousness which the Lord shall give me at that day and not to me only but unto all them also that love his appearing."
-ll Timothy 4:6-8

"And God hath both raised up the Lord, and will also raise up us by his own power."
-l Corinthians 6:14

"For we brought nothing into this world, and it is certain we carry nothing out."
-l Timothy 6:7

"Whereas ye know not what shall be on the morrow, for what is your life? It is even a vapour, that appeareth for a little time and then vanisheth away."
-James 4:14

"As the body without the spirit is dead, so faith without works is dead also."
-James 2:26

"Wherefore lay apart all filthiness and superfluity of naughtiness, and receive with meekness the engrafted word, which is able to save your soul."
-James 1:21

"And this is the record, that God hath given to us eternal life and this life is his Son."
-l John 5:11

"My flesh and my heart fail; But God is the strength of my heart."
-Psalm 73:26

"I am not alone because the Father is with me."
-John 16:32

"I have learned in whatever state I am, to be content."
-Philippians 4:11

"As the body without the spirit is dead, so faith without works is dead also."
-James 2:26

"For we must all appear before the judgment seat of Christ; that everyone may receive the things done in his body, according to that he hath done, whether it be good or bad."
-ll Corinthians 5:1

8. LIGHT

ROAD MAP brings value to you and will enhance your conscience which is the light of your soul. The Lord's words have taught me through my varied life that I can help others each day.

"For the life was manifested, and we have seen it, and bear witness and shew unto you that eternal life, which was with the father, and was manifested unto us."
-l John 1:2

"This then is the message which we have heard of him and declare unto you, that God is light and in him is no darkness at all."
-l John 1:5

"Then Jesus said unto them, Yet a little while is the light with you. Walk while ye have the light, lest darkness come upon you: for he that walketh in darkness knoweth not whither he goeth."

"While ye have light, believe in the light, that ye may be the children of light."
-John 12: 35 & 36

"But if we walk in the light, as he is in the light, we have fellowship with one another and the blood of Christ his Son cleanset us from all sin.

If we confess our sins, he is faithful and just to forgive us our sins and cleanse us from all unrighteouness"
-l John 1:5-9

" I am the light of the world. He who follows me shall not walk in darkness, but have the light of life."
-John 8:12

"The Lord will be a shelter for his people."
-Joel 3:16

"In him was life, and the life was the light of man."
-John 1:4

"You are the light of the world.... let your light so shine before others that they may see your good works and glorify your father in heaven."
-Matthew 5: 14-16

"The entrance of your words gives light."
-Psalm 119:130

"All the forces of darkness cannot stop what has ordained"
-Isaiah 14:27

9. HEAVEN

We know Jesus Christ will meet us at our death on earth, we, Christians, go straight into heaven into the presence of Jesus. We will give an accounting of our lives on earth, good and bad, Jesus will judge us accordingly and recommend to the Holy Father , we be admitted into his kingdom. Then Jesus will escort us to our heavenly mansion he had prepared for us. We will see again our loved ones and spend eternity with all members of heaven and do God's will in heaven.

What a joy to know some day we will wake up in the heavenly Father's presence and know the burdens of life are over. All our questions will be answered and all our fears and sorrows will be gone. Heaven's door is open to us.

"For as the heaven is high above the earth."
-Psalm 103:11

"For we know that if our earthly house of this tabernacle were dissolved, we have a building of God, an house not made with hands, eternal in the heavens."
-ll Corinthians 5:1

"In my Father's house are many mansions. If it were not so, I would have told you so. I go to prepare a place for you."
-John 14:2

"If I go and prepare a place for you, I will come again."
-John 14:3

"I am the way, the truth, and the life. No one comes to the Father except through me."
-John 14:6

"Verily, Verily, I say unto you, if a man keep my saying, he shall never see death."
-John 8:51

"I am the resurrection and the life. He who believes in me shall never die. Believest thou this."
-John 11:25-26

"God has given us eternal life, and this life is in his son."
-l John 5:11-12

"Someday our dead bodies will be raised in glory. And we will be like Christ in his resurrected body."
-l Corinthians 15:43

"For our citizenship is in heaven from which we eagerly wait for the Savior, the Lord Jesus Christ, who will transform our lowly body to conform with his heavenly body."
-Philippians 3:20-21

"God has given us eternal life, and this life is in his son."
-l John 5:11-12

"Because Christ is alive, we have an inheritance, incorruptible and undefiled...reserved in heaven."
-1 Peter 1:4

"Not everyone that saith unto me, Lord, Lord shall enter into the kingdom of heaven; but he that doeth the will of my father which is in heaven. Many will say to me in that day, have we not prophesied in thy name? and in thy name cast out devils? And in thy name done many wonderful works? And then will I profess unto them, I never knew you. Depart from me, ye that work iniquity."
-Matthew 7:21-23

"And these shall go away into everlasting punishment: But the righteous into life eternal."
-Matthew 25:46

"That if thou shalt confess with thy mouth, the Lord Jesus, and shalt believe in thine heart that god hath raised him from the dead, thou shalt be saved."
-Romans 10:9

"And the Lord shall deliver me from every evil work, and will preserve me unto his heavenly kingdom: To whom be glory for ever and ever. Amen."
-ll Timothy 4:18

"Blessed is the man that endureth temptation: for when he is tried, he shall receive the crown of life, which the Lord hath promised to them that love him."
-James 1:12

"For the Kingdom of God is not meat and drink; but righteousness and peace, and joy in the Holy Ghost."
-Romans 14:17"

"Therefore if any man be in Christ, he is a new creature; old things are passed away; behold, all things become new."
-ll Corinthians 5:17

"God shall wipe away all tears from their eyes."
-Revelation 7:17

"For in the resurrection they neither marry, nor are given in marriage, but are as the angels of God in heaven."
-Matthew 23:30

"...the resurrection from the dead, neither marry, nor are given in marriage."
-Matthew 20:35-36

"He that overcometh, the same shall be clothed in white rainment; and I will not blot out his name out of the book of life, but I will confers his name before my Father, and before his angels."
-Revelation 3:5

"...To him that overcometh will I give to eat of the tree of life, which is in the midst of the paradise of God."
-Revelation 2:7

"To him that overcometh will I grant to sit with me in my throne, even as I also overcame and am set down with my father in his throne."
-Revelation 3:21

"His servant shall serve him."
-Revelation 22:3

"I will never leave you nor forsake you."
-Hebrews 13:5

"I will give you rest."
-Matthew 11:28

"If we ask, anything according to his will, he hears us."
-l John 5:14

"God himself will be with them."
-Revelation 21:3

"Servant shall serve him."
-Revelation 22:3

"I am with you always to the very end of the world."
-Matthew 28:20

"Your throne, O God, is forever and ever."
-Psalm 45:6

"And these shall go away into everlasting punishment: But the righteous into life eternal."
-Matthew 25:46

"...............I will dwell in the House of the Lord forever."
-23 Psalm

10. ANGELS

Satan is a fallen angel. He transforms himself into an angel of light. He deceives everyone. Lucifer, his name, rebelled against God in heaven and wanted to take over. God threw him and all his brigade of devil angels out of heaven forever.

Earthly angels formed by God are sent to earth to protect us from Satan's evil devilish angels. Pray and ask the Holy Father, God, to rid Satan and all his evil angels and demons to flee your soul, body, family, home, work, church, school, and everything your involved with. Guaranteed, they all immediately flee elsewhere.

"He will give his angels charge of you, to guard you in all your ways."
-Psalm 91:11

"Let your light shine before men, that they may see your God works and glorify your Father in Heaven."
-Matthew 5:16

"Likewise, I say unto you, there is joy in the presence of the angels of God over one sinner that repented."
-Luke 15:10

"And to you who are troubled rest with us when the Lord Jesus shall be revealed from heaven with his mighty angels.

In flaming fire taking vengeance on them that know not God and that obey not the gospel of our Lord Jesus Christ.

Who shall be punished with everlasting destruction from the presence of the Lord, and, from the glory of his power."
-ll Thessalonians 1:7,8,9

"For God spared not the angels that sinned, but cast them down to hell, and delivered them into chains of darkness, to be reserved unto judgment."
-ll Peter 2:4

"Are they not all ministering spirits, sent forth to minister for them who shall be heirs of salvation?"
-Hebrews1:14

"Who is gone into heaven, and is on the right hand of God; angels and authorities and powers being made subject unto him."

"Likewise, I say unto you, there is joy in the presence of the angels of God over one sinner that repenteth."
-Luke 15:10

"And shall cast them into the furnace of fire: there shall be wailing and gnashing of teeth."
-Matthew 13:50

11. CONSCIENCE

I, Chuck Cotton, desire to rid my heart of any and all malice towards others. I also want to clear my sub-consciousness of any hurt I have caused anyone in my past.

The human conscience is defiled by sin. The Holy spirit can clean our conscience and rid satan by asking God to do so.

"I, myself, always strive to have a conscience without offense toward God and men."
-Acts 24:16

"Light of the soul God gives to steer me from evil toward God. God's word make us aware to moral and spiritual danger. God has given our conscience to us. He leads us in paths of righteousness for his name's sake."
-Psalm 23:3

"Pray for us for we trust we have a good conscience, in all things willing to live honestly."
-Hebrews 13:18

We must make a valid repentance to turn away from sin and a conscience decision making a commitment to follow the Lord's will.

12. DISCIPLINE

The Lord giveth and the Lord taketh away. His discipline on us confirms his love for us. Always practice God's will.

"Correct thy son, and he shall give thee rest, yea, he shall give delight unto thy soul."
-Proverbs 29:17

"Thou shalt also consider in thine heart, that, as a man chasteneth his son, so the Lord thy God chasteneth thee."

"Therefore, thou shalt keep the commandments of the Lord thy God to walk in his ways, and to fear him."
-Deuteronomy 8: 5-6

"Behold, Happy is the man whom God correcteth; therefore despise not thou the chastening of the almighty."
-Job 5:17

"Train up a child in the way he should go: and when he is old, he will not depart from it."
-Proverbs 22:6

"A good man leaveth an inheritance to his children's children: and the wealth of the sinner is laid up for the just."
-Proverbs 13:22

"For Moses said, honour thy father and thy mother, and, whoever curseth father or mother, let, him die the death."
-Mark 7:10

13. MARRIAGE

When you marry, you commit your lives to each and become one. If blessed with children, God's will is to raise those precious children the right way.

People deeply in love find absolute bliss simply being in each other's presence.

God hates divorce. We are blessed.

"Wherefore they are no more twain, but one flesh. What therefore God had joined together, let not man put asunder."
-Matthew 19:6

"The children of the world marry, and are given in marriage."
-Luke 20:34

"What therefore God hath joined together, let not man put asunder."
-Mark 10:9

"That their hearts might be comforted, being knit together in love, and unto all riches of the full assurances of understanding, to the acknowledgement of the mystery of God, and the father, and of Christ."
-Colossians 2:2

"A virtuous woman is a crown to her husband: But she that maketh ashamed, is a rottenness in his bones."
-Proverbs 12:4

"Whoso findeth a wife findeth a good thing and obtaineth favour of the Lord."
-Proverbs 18:22

"Laying up in store for themselves a good foundation against the time to come, that they may lay hold on eternal life."
-l Timothy 6:19

14. ABORTION

LIFE BEGINS AT CONCEPTION. JESUS WAS CONCEIVED BY THE HOLY GHOST IN MARY'S WOMB. GOD COMMANDS THOU SHALL NOT KILL. ABORTION IS MURDER. THOSE WHO PRACTICE INFANTICIDE, HARVEST BABY PARTS AND DESTROYS OUR CHRISTIAN BIRTHRIGHT ARE CAST INTO HELL.

"If men strive; and hurt a woman with a child, so that her fruit depart from her....he will be surely punished."
-Exodus 21:22

"Even so it is not the will of your father which is in heaven, that one of these little ones should perish."
-Matthew 18:14

"Even everyone that is called by my name, for I have created him for my glory: I have formed him, yea, I have made him."
-Isaiah 43:7

"Lo, children are an heritage of the Lord: and the fruit of the womb is his reward."
-Psalm 127:3

"For the children being not yet born, neither having done any good or evil, that the purpose of God according to election might stand not of works, but of him that calleth."
-Romans 9:11

"But thou art he that took me out of the womb: thou didst make the hope when I was upon my mother's breast."

"I was cast upon thee from the womb: thou art my God from my mother's belly."
-Psalm 22:9-10

"Before I formed thee in the belly I knew thee, and before thou comest forth out of the womb I sanctified thee a prophet unto the nations."
-Jeremiah 1:5

"For thou hast possessed my reins: thou hast covered me in my mother's womb."

"I will praise thee; for I am fearfully and wonderfully made: marvellous are thy works; and my soul knoweth right well."
-Psalm 139:13-14

"But when it pleased God, who separated me from my mother's womb, and called me by his grace."
-Galatians 1:15

15. HATRED

Satan focuses on hate strategy to take us down because we believe in Jesus Christ as the Son of God. There is so much hate in our society and throughout the world like never before in history. This hate is spearheaded by Satan and his devilish brigade of evil doers. The world is in a mixed state of confusion and scorn over culture, race, pagan politics, education, government, liberty, constitutions, rule of law all resulting in hate.

Youth are rebelling against God. Jesus says the problems are within us. We are rejecting God's plan. Youth are in full revolt against all religions. Unending misery has set in with young people but can end by repenting and receiving Christ.

GOD DEMANDS WE LOVE EACH OTHER.

"If a man says, I love God, and hateth his brother, he is a liar: for he that loveth not his brother whom he hath seen, how can he love God whom he hath not seen."
-l John 4: 20

"A false witness shall not be unpunished, and he that speaketh lies shall perish."
-Proverbs 19:9

"If the world hate you, ye know that it hated me before it hated you."
-John 15:16

"The Lord trieth the righteous: but the wicked and him that loveth violence his soul hateth."
-Psalm 11:5

"Consider mine enemies; for they are many, and they hate me with cruel hatred."
-Psalm 25:19

"He that hateth me hateth my Father also."
-John 15:23

"Where hatred rules, love is crowded out."
-Psalm 109

"For the mouth of the wicked and the mouth of the deceitful are opened against me; they have spoken against me with a lying tongue. They have compassed me also with words of hatred; about and fought against me without a cause."
-Psalm 109:2,3

"And ye shall be hated of all men for my name's sake but he that endureth to the end shall be saved."
-Matthew 10:22

"Bless them which persecute you; bless, and curse not."
-Romans 12:14

"A double minded man is unstable in all his ways."
-James 1:8

"But the tongue can no man tame; it is an unruly evil, full of deadly poison."
-James 3:8

"That they which do such things shall not inherit the kingdom of God."
-Galatians 6:20,21

GOD WILL NOT ALLOW PEOPLE FILLED WITH HATRED TO LIVE IN HIS KINGDOM.

16. BUSINESS

Every headline, every news report confirms what the prophet Jeremiah said centuries ago, "The heart is deceitful above all things, and desperately wicked; who can know it."
-Jeremiah 17:9

I had the privilege working for myself developing faith-based businesses. Yes, there was a price attached to the privileges, but being with your children before and after school and watching them grow up was a great reward from the Lord. Life is short and soon over but after the heavy burdens we have carried, it will seem trivial then.

Thousands of messages rain down on us daily attempting to shape our thinking-TV, E-mail, social media, junk mail, video, movies, commercials, billboards, conversation and newspapers.

Just an endless barrage of information mostly influenced by satan and his brigade. My college journalism professor at SIU-Carbondale taught us "RESPONSIBLE JOURNALISM IS TELLING THE TRUTH."

"A double-minded man is unstable in all ways."
-James 1:8

Only God can shape our thinking. Praying unlocks the doors of heaven and releases the power of God. Praying on your knees is the most powerful weapon ever developed.

"Rejoice always, pray without ceasing."
-l Thessalonians 5:16-17

"You call me teacher and Lord, and you say well, for I so I am."
-John 13:13

"You do not have because you do not ask."
-James 4:2

"Ask, and it shall be given to you; seek, and ye shall find; knock, and it shall be opened unto you."
-Matthew 7:7

"For everyone that asketh receiveth; and he that seeketh findeth; and to him that knocketh, it shall be opened."
-Matthew 7:8

"What will it profit a man if he gains the whole world, and loses his own soul?"
-Mark 8:36

"For the love of money is the root of all evil."
-l Timothy 6:10

"The laborer is worthy of his reward."
-l Timothy 5:18

"And that ye study to be quiet, and to do your own business, and to work with your own hands, as we commanded you."
-l Thessalonians 4:11

"That no man goes beyond and defraud his brother in any matter: Because the Lord is the avenger of all such, as we have also forewarned you and testified."
- l Thessalonians 4:6

"Rob not the poor, because he is poor."
-Proverbs 22:22

"Beware of false prophets, which come to you in sheep's clothing, but inwardly, they are ravening wolves."
-Matthew 7:15

"At the end of every seven years, thou shalt make a release."

"And this is the manner of the release: Every creditor that lendeth ought unto his neighbor shall release it. He shall not exact it of his neighbor or his brother; because it is called the Lord's release."
-Deuteronomy 15:1-2

"He that putteth not out his money to usury, nor taketh reward against the innocent. He that doeth these things, shall never be moved."
-Psalm 15:5

"If thou lend money to any of my people that is poor by thee thou shall be to him an usurer, neither shalt thou lay upon him usury."
-Exodus 22:25

"That no man go beyond and defraud his brother in any matter: because the Lord is the avenger of all such, as we also have forewarned you and testified."
-1 Thessalonians 4:6

17. AMBASSADOR

God has taught you something through your trials that could help someone else today.

Our mission as we age is to do purpose in recruiting, training and preparing others for eternity. Christ calls us to live under his authority and the scriptures. The world seeks holy men and women who live under Christ's authority. Disbelievers won't listen unless we back it up with the way we live.

ASK YOURSELF, ARE YOU AN AMBASSADOR FOR CHRIST?

Pledge yourself to our Lord to be an ambassador for Christ.

"We are ambassadors for Christ."
-ll Corinthians 5:20, 5:6-8

"Now then we are ambassadors for Christ , as though God did beseech you by us; We pray you in Christ's stead, be ye reconciled to God."
-ll Corinthians 20

18. THANKS

My 94-year old Grandmother Phillips always said that one of the greatest sins was that of ingratitude. Salvation is free, Jesus Christ paid for it in full.

"Thanks be to God for his indescribable gift."
-ll Corinthians 9:15

"In everything give thanks: for this is the will of God in Christ Jesus concerning you."
-l Thessalonians 5:18

"And let the peace of God rule in your hearts, to the which also ye are called and be ye thankful."
-Colossians 3:15

"Give and it will be given to you."
-Luke 6:58

An angel came to give Jesus strength facing the horror of the crucifixion.

"He had give thanks."
-Matthew 15:36

"Whatsoever ye shall ask the Father in my name, he will give it to you."
-John 16:24

"Giving thanks always for all things unto God and the Father in the name of Lord Jesus Christ."
-Ephesians 5:20

Always give your best to every friend God places in your life. Express thanks when friends are helpful.

19. FAVORITES

Christ offers

"A kingdom which can not be shaken."
-Hebrews 12:28

God has prepared a perfect place for us in heaven.

Your next breath is a gift from the Lord.

"Gain a heart of wisdom."
-Psalm 90:12

"If I go and prepare a place for you, I will come again."
-John 14:3

"I am the way, the truth, and the life, no comes to the Father except through me."
-John 14:6

"Because Christ is alive, we have an inheritance incorruptible and undefiled...reserved in heaven."
-l Peter 1:4

"Let your light so shine before men, that they may see your good deeds and praise your father in heaven."
-Matthew 5:16

"The fruit of the spirit is love, joy, peace,....gentleness, self-control."
-Galatians 5:22-23

"You do not know what will happen tomorrow."
-James 4:14

Road Map

The word of God tells us what to believe and how to live. The Holy Spirit inspired the Bible authors. "All scripture is given by inspiration of God, and is profitable for doctrine, for reproof, for correction, for instruction is righteousness."
-ll Timothy 3:16

REGARDLESS WHO YOU ARE, YOU ARE A HUMAN BEING, ONE BLOOD, WHETHER MALE, FEMALE, CREED, RACE, BODIES, CULTURE, RELIGION- A GIFT FROM GOD.

"And hath made of one blood all nations of men for to dwell on all the face of the earth."
-Acts 17:26

"Let every soul be subject unto the higher powers. For there is no power but of God. The powers that be are ordained of God."
-Romans 14:1

"For the truth's sake which dwelleth in us and shall be with us forever."
-ll John 1:2

"Grace be with you, mercy and peace, from God the Father, and from the Lord Jesus Christ, the Son of the Father, in Truth and Love."
-ll John 7:3

"I will give them one heart and I will put a new spirit within you; and I will take the stony heart out their flesh, and will give them a heart of flesh."
-Ezekiel 11:19

"That ye might walk worthy of the Lord unto all pleasing being fruitful in every good work, and increasing in the knowledge of God."
-Colossians 1:10

"Seek those things which are above, where Christ is."
-Colossians 3:1

"Come to me…and I will give you rest."
-Matthew 11:28

"The testing of your faith produces patience."
-James 1:3

"Do not be afraid."
-Matthew 28:10

"First, Seek the Kingdom of God…and all these things shall be added to you."
-Matthew 6:33

"No one comes to the father except through me."
-John 14:6

"That thou thyself also walkest orderly, and keepest the law."
-Acts 21:24

"And if a house be divided against itself that house cannot stand."
-Mark 3:25

"Teaching us that, denying ungodliness and wordly lusts, we should live soberly, righteously, and Godly, in this present world."
-Titus 2:12

"With God all things are possible."
-Matthew 19:26

"For bodily exercise profiteth little: but godliness is profitable unto all things, having promise of the life that now is, and of that which is close."
-l Timothy 4:8

"Therefore, do not be anxious about tomorrow for tomorrow will be anxious for itself. Let the day's own trouble be sufficient for the day."
-Matthew 6:34

"Prove all things; hold fast that which is good."
-l Thessalonians 5:21 -The 12 disciples were:

Simon Peter, Andrew, James, John, Philip, Bartholomew, Thomas, Matthew, James, Thaddaeus, Simon, Judas.
-Matthew 10:1-4

"Love the Lord your God with all your heart….and your neighbor as yourself."
-Luke 10:27

20. CONCLUSION

Wherever life has taken you, you need to spark your life for its remainder on earth.

God gave you all the resources to do his will, your body, talent, and energy, - and he showered you with gifts and blessings.

Sparks ignite that fire in your belly and makes you come alive.

Sparks give you a sense of liveliness, excitement, spirituality, and confidence.

Sparks bring you joy and hope.

However, the devil and his brigade are constantly attempting to extinguish those sparks and cause: lifelessness, inactivity, brain fog, feebleness, spiritlessness, stupidity, cowardice, even death. Everyone on earth is faced with the evil, satanic revolutions of culture change, religious, and political change.

Sparks are a magnetic chemistry between you and Jesus Christ. ROAD MAP is a new day for you. Make a U-turn and turn that spark into sparks. Pray for Jesus to change your life, especially those who are non-believers. Jesus took our sins to the cross and took the right road to bring us to God, his heavenly father.

Starting my life, I quickly had gotten off the path and realized I needed a road map to find my way. Many citizens are lost and need a ROAD MAP to arrive at their destination.

SO WHO NEEDS A ROAD MAP?

EVERYONE

Whether you are a student, athlete, coach, business person, politician, parent, grandparent, senior citizen, employee- Don't regret growing old. It is a privilege denied to many. Be prepared to end your life right. Many people are in deep sin and will say they wish they had never fallen into such sin. They know they are completely lost and do not know which way to go. Some people want to find a way to go forward but need a Road Map. Some people just don't care and are wanderers and nomads. Many people just don't think they need a ROAD MAP or anything.

As the aging reality sinks in, people ask "Where Did My Life Go?" I'm lost. I'm gambling my soul. I know I'll lose if I don't change. The ROAD MAP will guide you to your final destination- Heaven's gates. It is not too late-commit to Christ- seek a pure heart cleansed by the Holy Spirit and the word of God. Find a solitude place and get on your knees, pray to Jesus, and repent your sins and ask him to forgive each and every sin you have committed. Ask him to come into your life. He will provide your road map ensuring the way to him. The cross will ever remain the unchanging grounds of forgiveness. If you do so, you will not see death but immediately enter a new dimension having eternal life with our Lord and your loved ones. My ROAD MAP encourages you to live each day as if it is your last. Someday it will be and your soul will be saved.

"COME NEAR TO GOD AND HE WILL COME NEAR TO YOU."
- James 4:8

21. SPECIAL RECOGNITION

I WISH TO GIVE SPECIAL RECOGNITION TO MY FRIEND, JERMAINE BIRDOW aka "Bird".

Jermaine worked for me part time as a limousine detailer, while attending Oklahoma State University. He was a star linebacker for the football team. He was projected as a first-round draft choice for the Dallas Cowboys. Bird, unfortunately stubbed his toe and committed a crime just prior to the draft. He was incarcerated for 18 years. During this period, with his son, Taven, he coached from his cell. Taven was All-State and led the state in rushing yards. He was offered several scholarships and chose the Air Force Academy. He was the fullback on the football team and graduated with honors. His dad, "Bird" raised him from that cell the best he could.

I never abandoned "Bird" while in prison and supported him in every way I could. I knew his heart, his soul, his pulse, and his faith in Jesus Christ as his savior. "Bird" was a 22 year old black man who with two middle east guys made a mistake and caught in an attempted robbery right after 9/11 World Trade Center attack. These fellows were thought of as terrorists and the judicial system sentenced them to sixty years. Nothing was taken in the attempted robbery which was another middle Eastern family that allegedly had a safe with lots of money in their home, whom the other two middle eastern guys knew. The wife called the police and they surrendered. However, "Bird" tagged along with his friends admittedly made a serious mistake and paid for his mistake. I knew gross injustice had been carried out in such a long sentence. Through the years and several attorneys, the sentence was reduced to 18 years.

I quote a most important biblical verse:

"Naked, and ye clothe me; I was sick, and ye visited me: I was in prison, and ye came unto me."
-Matthew 25:36

I never abandoned "Bird" and today, I wish to tell you of his most worthy accomplishments in establishing himself in society.

When released from prison, naturally, he was naive about so many things. His physical specimen is a fellow, 6 FT 5 IN, 260 LB, and not an ounce of fat on him. Knowing his potential, I told him he has a good 50 years in front of him and I committed to him, I would help him realize and reach his potential.

On his own, "Bird", having the entrepreneurial spirit, is a lecturer for the FCA (Fellowship of Christian America.) He started a yard maintenance business with the purchase of a used lawn mower and has grown his business into a major mowing/landscaping operation all by himself with no financial help. He has paid off his prison debt, purchase a vehicle, a truck and trailer, as well as equipment. I expect great things from "Bird" as he is tremendous motivational speaker, humorist, and a Christian. I am sharing with his permission of course, his poem, I ASKED GOD.

I ASKED God what is love…

And He said: LOVE IS ME

I said with all that goes on in this world today, I find it hard to agree…

HE SAID THAT MY LOVE NEVER FAILS, AND THAT YOU WILL COME TO SEE

I asked God for favor

HE SAID, OH YES YOU CAN

Road Map

I asked God for wisdom…

HE SAID, PATIENCE YOUNG MAN

I asked God for grace…

HE SAID THAT GRACE ABOUNDS

I asked him again…

HE SAID OH HOW SWEET THE SOUND

I asked God for mercy…

HE SAID MY MERCY NEVER ENDS

Well: what about compassion…

HE SAID I CALL YOU FRIEND

I asked God what is life…

HE SAID LIFE IS ETERNITY

I asked God how to receive life….

HE SAID CHRIST IS THE KEY

I asked God for help

HE SAID COME UNTO ME

I asked God to move mountains…

HE SAID, I NEED YOU TO BELIEVE.

I said I can't, my heart is broken, I'm in need of surgery.

HE SAID, I SPECIALIZE IN THE HEART

AND I CAN FIX THEM FOR FREE.

I said, I'M ASHAMED, UNWORTHY, AND YOU SEE MY LIFE IS TRULY A MESS

He said, I give beauty for ashes, and what teacher doesn't prepare for a test?

All my thought, failures, and insecurities, you know I'm never precise…

He simply smiled and said, TRUST IN ME and I know He said it twice.

I said, "At the end of life's journey, GOD, What does all of this really mean?"

Keep the faith and in all things give thanks and keep your crown to give back to the KING.

I asked God to Bless you

Jermaine Birdow # 33

Printed in the USA
CPSIA information can be obtained
at www.ICGtesting.com
JSHW020851010424
60081JS00001B/75

9 781639 451005